This Journal
belongs to

_____

Vision Board

My top 3

I want to do...	I want to learn...
1.	1.
2.	2.
3.	3.

I want to be...	I want to try...
1.	1.
2.	2.
3.	3.

I want to start...	I want to give...
1.	1.
2.	2.
3.	3.

AFFIRMATION OF THE WEEK:

I FEEL …

BECAUSE…

MY WEEK WAS…

TO DO

REMINDERS & NOTES:

a week of *gratitude* ♥

I AM GRATEFUL FOR ...

_____
_____
_____

I AM GRATEFUL FOR ...

_____
_____
_____

I AM GRATEFUL FOR ...

_____
_____
_____

I AM GRATEFUL FOR ...

_____
_____
_____

I AM GRATEFUL FOR ...

_____
_____
_____

I AM GRATEFUL FOR ...

_____
_____
_____

I AM GRATEFUL FOR ...

_____
_____
_____

WHAT I LEARNED THIS WEEK

_____
_____
_____

Self-Care Check-in

TICK THE BOXES OF THE ACTIVITIES YOU DO TO TAKE CARE OF YOURSELF.

- ☐ Eat three main meals
- ☐ Go on a 24-hr social media detox
- ☐ Find a quiet spot to meditate
- ☐ Light an aromatic candle
- ☐ Do a gratitude list
- ☐ Practice deep breathing
- ☐ Exercise
- ☐ Cuddle a pet or someone you love
- ☐ Visit a family member
- ☐ Spend time outdoors
- ☐ Go for a bath or a long shower
- ☐ Listen to good music
- ☐ Catch up with a friend
- ☐ Try something new

AFFIRMATION OF THE WEEK:

I FEEL ...

TO DO

BECAUSE...

MY WEEK WAS...

REMINDERS & NOTES:

a week of *gratitude* ♥

I AM GRATEFUL FOR ...

_____
_____
_____

I AM GRATEFUL FOR ...

_____
_____
_____

I AM GRATEFUL FOR ...

_____
_____
_____

I AM GRATEFUL FOR ...

_____
_____
_____

I AM GRATEFUL FOR ...

_____
_____
_____

I AM GRATEFUL FOR ...

_____
_____
_____

I AM GRATEFUL FOR ...

_____
_____
_____

WHAT I LEARNED THIS WEEK

_____
_____
_____

my bucket list

if you only had a month to live, what would you do?

☐
☐
☐
☐
☐
☐
☐
☐
☐
☐
☐
☐
☐
☐

AFFIRMATION OF THE WEEK:

I FEEL ...

BECAUSE...

MY WEEK WAS...

TO DO

REMINDERS & NOTES:

a week of gratitude

I AM GRATEFUL FOR ...

_____
_____
_____

I AM GRATEFUL FOR ...

_____
_____
_____

I AM GRATEFUL FOR ...

_____
_____
_____

I AM GRATEFUL FOR ...

_____
_____
_____

I AM GRATEFUL FOR ...

_____
_____
_____

I AM GRATEFUL FOR ...

_____
_____
_____

I AM GRATEFUL FOR ...

_____
_____
_____

WHAT I LEARNED THIS WEEK

_____
_____
_____

Just like the moon, we go through phases...

AFFIRMATION OF THE WEEK:

I FEEL ...

TO DO

-
-
-
-
-

BECAUSE...

MY WEEK WAS...

REMINDERS & NOTES:

a week of gratitude

I AM GRATEFUL FOR ...

I AM GRATEFUL FOR ...

I AM GRATEFUL FOR ...

I AM GRATEFUL FOR ...

I AM GRATEFUL FOR ...

I AM GRATEFUL FOR ...

I AM GRATEFUL FOR ...

WHAT I LEARNED THIS WEEK

New things to try...

when was the last time you did something for the first time ...?

- ☐ STAND UP PADDLING
- ☐ YOGA COURSE
- ☐ DANCE LESSON
- ☐
- ☐
- ☐
- ☐
- ☐
- ☐

AFFIRMATION OF THE WEEK:

I FEEL ...

TO DO

BECAUSE...

MY WEEK WAS...

REMINDERS & NOTES:

a week of gratitude ♥

I AM GRATEFUL FOR ...

I AM GRATEFUL FOR ...

I AM GRATEFUL FOR ...

I AM GRATEFUL FOR ...

I AM GRATEFUL FOR ...

I AM GRATEFUL FOR ...

I AM GRATEFUL FOR ...

WHAT I LEARNED THIS WEEK

My top 5 life goals

AFFIRMATION OF THE WEEK:

I FEEL ...

TO DO

BECAUSE...

MY WEEK WAS...

REMINDERS & NOTES:

a week of gratitude ♥

I AM GRATEFUL FOR ...

I AM GRATEFUL FOR ...

I AM GRATEFUL FOR ...

I AM GRATEFUL FOR ...

I AM GRATEFUL FOR ...

I AM GRATEFUL FOR ...

I AM GRATEFUL FOR ...

WHAT I LEARNED THIS WEEK

AFFIRMATION OF THE WEEK:

I FEEL ...

TO DO

BECAUSE...

MY WEEK WAS...

REMINDERS & NOTES:

a week of *gratitude* ♥

I AM GRATEFUL FOR …

_____
_____
_____

I AM GRATEFUL FOR …

_____
_____
_____

I AM GRATEFUL FOR …

_____
_____
_____

I AM GRATEFUL FOR …

_____
_____
_____

I AM GRATEFUL FOR …

_____
_____
_____

I AM GRATEFUL FOR …

_____
_____
_____

I AM GRATEFUL FOR …

_____
_____
_____

WHAT I LEARNED THIS WEEK

_____
_____
_____

AFFIRMATION OF THE WEEK:

I FEEL ...

TO DO

-
-
-
-
-

BECAUSE...

MY WEEK WAS...

REMINDERS & NOTES:

a week of gratitude ♥

I AM GRATEFUL FOR ...

I AM GRATEFUL FOR ...

I AM GRATEFUL FOR ...

I AM GRATEFUL FOR ...

I AM GRATEFUL FOR ...

I AM GRATEFUL FOR ...

I AM GRATEFUL FOR ...

WHAT I LEARNED THIS WEEK

AFFIRMATION OF THE WEEK:

I FEEL ...

TO DO

BECAUSE...

MY WEEK WAS...

REMINDERS & NOTES:

a week of gratitude

I AM GRATEFUL FOR ...

I AM GRATEFUL FOR ...

I AM GRATEFUL FOR ...

I AM GRATEFUL FOR ...

I AM GRATEFUL FOR ...

I AM GRATEFUL FOR ...

I AM GRATEFUL FOR ...

WHAT I LEARNED THIS WEEK

AFFIRMATION OF THE WEEK:

I FEEL ...   TO DO

BECAUSE...

MY WEEK WAS...

REMINDERS & NOTES:

a week of *gratitude* ♥

I AM GRATEFUL FOR ...

I AM GRATEFUL FOR ...

I AM GRATEFUL FOR ...

I AM GRATEFUL FOR ...

I AM GRATEFUL FOR ...

I AM GRATEFUL FOR ...

I AM GRATEFUL FOR ...

WHAT I LEARNED THIS WEEK

AFFIRMATION OF THE WEEK:

I FEEL ...

BECAUSE...

MY WEEK WAS...

TO DO

REMINDERS & NOTES:

a week of *gratitude* ♥

I AM GRATEFUL FOR ...

_____
_____
_____

I AM GRATEFUL FOR ...

_____
_____
_____

I AM GRATEFUL FOR ...

_____
_____
_____

I AM GRATEFUL FOR ...

_____
_____
_____

I AM GRATEFUL FOR ...

_____
_____
_____

I AM GRATEFUL FOR ...

_____
_____
_____

WHAT I LEARNED THIS WEEK

_____
_____
_____

AFFIRMATION OF THE WEEK:

I FEEL ...

TO DO

BECAUSE...

MY WEEK WAS...

REMINDERS & NOTES:

a week of gratitude

I AM GRATEFUL FOR ...

I AM GRATEFUL FOR ...

I AM GRATEFUL FOR ...

I AM GRATEFUL FOR ...

I AM GRATEFUL FOR ...

I AM GRATEFUL FOR ...

I AM GRATEFUL FOR ...

WHAT I LEARNED THIS WEEK

AFFIRMATION OF THE WEEK:

I FEEL ...

TO DO

BECAUSE...

MY WEEK WAS...

REMINDERS & NOTES:

a week of gratitude

I AM GRATEFUL FOR ...

I AM GRATEFUL FOR ...

I AM GRATEFUL FOR ...

I AM GRATEFUL FOR ...

I AM GRATEFUL FOR ...

I AM GRATEFUL FOR ...

I AM GRATEFUL FOR ...

WHAT I LEARNED THIS WEEK

AFFIRMATION OF THE WEEK:

I FEEL ...

TO DO

BECAUSE...

MY WEEK WAS...

REMINDERS & NOTES:

a week of *gratitude* ♥

I AM GRATEFUL FOR ...

_____
_____
_____

I AM GRATEFUL FOR ...

_____
_____
_____

I AM GRATEFUL FOR ...

_____
_____
_____

I AM GRATEFUL FOR ...

_____
_____
_____

I AM GRATEFUL FOR ...

_____
_____
_____

I AM GRATEFUL FOR ...

_____
_____
_____

I AM GRATEFUL FOR ...

_____
_____
_____

WHAT I LEARNED THIS WEEK

_____
_____
_____

AFFIRMATION OF THE WEEK:

I FEEL ...

TO DO

BECAUSE...

MY WEEK WAS...

REMINDERS & NOTES:

a week of *gratitude* ♥

I AM GRATEFUL FOR ...

_____
_____
_____

I AM GRATEFUL FOR ...

_____
_____
_____

I AM GRATEFUL FOR ...

_____
_____
_____

I AM GRATEFUL FOR ...

_____
_____
_____

I AM GRATEFUL FOR ...

_____
_____
_____

I AM GRATEFUL FOR ...

_____
_____
_____

I AM GRATEFUL FOR ...

_____
_____
_____

WHAT I LEARNED THIS WEEK

_____
_____
_____

AFFIRMATION OF THE WEEK:

I FEEL ...

TO DO

BECAUSE...

MY WEEK WAS...

REMINDERS & NOTES:

a week of gratitude

I AM GRATEFUL FOR ...

___
___
___

I AM GRATEFUL FOR ...

___
___
___

I AM GRATEFUL FOR ...

___
___
___

I AM GRATEFUL FOR ...

___
___
___

I AM GRATEFUL FOR ...

___
___
___

I AM GRATEFUL FOR ...

___
___
___

I AM GRATEFUL FOR ...

___
___
___

WHAT I LEARNED THIS WEEK

___
___
___

AFFIRMATION OF THE WEEK:

I FEEL ...

TO DO

BECAUSE...

MY WEEK WAS...

REMINDERS & NOTES:

a week of
gratitude ♥

I AM GRATEFUL FOR ...

I AM GRATEFUL FOR ...

I AM GRATEFUL FOR ...

I AM GRATEFUL FOR ...

I AM GRATEFUL FOR ...

I AM GRATEFUL FOR ...

I AM GRATEFUL FOR ...

WHAT I LEARNED THIS WEEK

AFFIRMATION OF THE WEEK:

I FEEL ...   TO DO

BECAUSE...

MY WEEK WAS...

REMINDERS & NOTES:

a week of gratitude

I AM GRATEFUL FOR ...

I AM GRATEFUL FOR ...

I AM GRATEFUL FOR ...

I AM GRATEFUL FOR ...

I AM GRATEFUL FOR ...

I AM GRATEFUL FOR ...

I AM GRATEFUL FOR ...

WHAT I LEARNED THIS WEEK

AFFIRMATION OF THE WEEK:

I FEEL ...

TO DO

BECAUSE...

MY WEEK WAS...

REMINDERS & NOTES:

a week of
gratitude ♥

I AM GRATEFUL FOR …

I AM GRATEFUL FOR …

I AM GRATEFUL FOR …

I AM GRATEFUL FOR …

I AM GRATEFUL FOR …

I AM GRATEFUL FOR …

I AM GRATEFUL FOR …

WHAT I LEARNED THIS WEEK

AFFIRMATION OF THE WEEK:

I FEEL ...

TO DO

BECAUSE...

MY WEEK WAS...

REMINDERS & NOTES:

a week of *gratitude* ♥

I AM GRATEFUL FOR ...

I AM GRATEFUL FOR ...

I AM GRATEFUL FOR ...

I AM GRATEFUL FOR ...

I AM GRATEFUL FOR ...

I AM GRATEFUL FOR ...

I AM GRATEFUL FOR ...

WHAT I LEARNED THIS WEEK

AFFIRMATION OF THE WEEK:

I FEEL ...

BECAUSE...

MY WEEK WAS...

TO DO

REMINDERS & NOTES:

a week of *gratitude* ♥

I AM GRATEFUL FOR …

I AM GRATEFUL FOR …

I AM GRATEFUL FOR …

I AM GRATEFUL FOR …

I AM GRATEFUL FOR …

I AM GRATEFUL FOR …

I AM GRATEFUL FOR …

WHAT I LEARNED THIS WEEK

AFFIRMATION OF THE WEEK:

I FEEL ...

TO DO

BECAUSE...

MY WEEK WAS...

REMINDERS & NOTES:

a week of gratitude

I AM GRATEFUL FOR ...

I AM GRATEFUL FOR ...

I AM GRATEFUL FOR ...

I AM GRATEFUL FOR ...

I AM GRATEFUL FOR ...

I AM GRATEFUL FOR ...

I AM GRATEFUL FOR ...

WHAT I LEARNED THIS WEEK

AFFIRMATION OF THE WEEK:

I FEEL ...

TO DO

BECAUSE...

MY WEEK WAS...

REMINDERS & NOTES:

a week of *gratitude* ♥

I AM GRATEFUL FOR ...

I AM GRATEFUL FOR ...

I AM GRATEFUL FOR ...

I AM GRATEFUL FOR ...

I AM GRATEFUL FOR ...

I AM GRATEFUL FOR ...

I AM GRATEFUL FOR ...

WHAT I LEARNED THIS WEEK

AFFIRMATION OF THE WEEK:

I FEEL ...

TO DO

BECAUSE...

MY WEEK WAS...

REMINDERS & NOTES:

a week of gratitude

I AM GRATEFUL FOR ...

I AM GRATEFUL FOR ...

I AM GRATEFUL FOR ...

I AM GRATEFUL FOR ...

I AM GRATEFUL FOR ...

I AM GRATEFUL FOR ...

I AM GRATEFUL FOR ...

WHAT I LEARNED THIS WEEK

AFFIRMATION OF THE WEEK:

I FEEL ...

TO DO

BECAUSE...

MY WEEK WAS...

REMINDERS & NOTES:

a week of *gratitude* ♥

I AM GRATEFUL FOR ...

I AM GRATEFUL FOR ...

I AM GRATEFUL FOR ...

I AM GRATEFUL FOR ...

I AM GRATEFUL FOR ...

I AM GRATEFUL FOR ...

I AM GRATEFUL FOR ...

WHAT I LEARNED THIS WEEK

AFFIRMATION OF THE WEEK:

I FEEL ...

TO DO

BECAUSE...

MY WEEK WAS...

REMINDERS & NOTES:

a week of gratitude ♥

I AM GRATEFUL FOR …

I AM GRATEFUL FOR …

I AM GRATEFUL FOR …

I AM GRATEFUL FOR …

I AM GRATEFUL FOR …

I AM GRATEFUL FOR …

I AM GRATEFUL FOR …

WHAT I LEARNED THIS WEEK

AFFIRMATION OF THE WEEK:

I FEEL ...

TO DO

BECAUSE...

MY WEEK WAS...

REMINDERS & NOTES:

a week of gratitude

I AM GRATEFUL FOR ...

I AM GRATEFUL FOR ...

I AM GRATEFUL FOR ...

I AM GRATEFUL FOR ...

I AM GRATEFUL FOR ...

I AM GRATEFUL FOR ...

I AM GRATEFUL FOR ...

WHAT I LEARNED THIS WEEK

AFFIRMATION OF THE WEEK:

I FEEL ...

TO DO

BECAUSE...

MY WEEK WAS...

REMINDERS & NOTES:

a week of *gratitude* ♥

I AM GRATEFUL FOR ...

_____
_____
_____

I AM GRATEFUL FOR ...

_____
_____
_____

I AM GRATEFUL FOR ...

_____
_____
_____

I AM GRATEFUL FOR ...

_____
_____
_____

I AM GRATEFUL FOR ...

_____
_____
_____

I AM GRATEFUL FOR ...

_____
_____
_____

I AM GRATEFUL FOR ...

_____
_____
_____

WHAT I LEARNED THIS WEEK

_____
_____
_____

AFFIRMATION OF THE WEEK:

I FEEL ...

TO DO

- [ ]
- [ ]
- [ ]
- [ ]
- [ ]
- [ ]

BECAUSE...

MY WEEK WAS...

REMINDERS & NOTES:

a week of gratitude

I AM GRATEFUL FOR ...

I AM GRATEFUL FOR ...

I AM GRATEFUL FOR ...

I AM GRATEFUL FOR ...

I AM GRATEFUL FOR ...

I AM GRATEFUL FOR ...

I AM GRATEFUL FOR ...

WHAT I LEARNED THIS WEEK

AFFIRMATION OF THE WEEK:

I FEEL ...

TO DO

BECAUSE...

MY WEEK WAS...

REMINDERS & NOTES:

a week of
gratitude ♥

I AM GRATEFUL FOR …

_____
_____
_____

I AM GRATEFUL FOR …

_____
_____
_____

I AM GRATEFUL FOR …

_____
_____
_____

I AM GRATEFUL FOR …

_____
_____
_____

I AM GRATEFUL FOR …

_____
_____
_____

I AM GRATEFUL FOR …

_____
_____
_____

I AM GRATEFUL FOR …

_____
_____
_____

WHAT I LEARNED THIS WEEK

_____
_____
_____

AFFIRMATION OF THE WEEK:

I FEEL ...

TO DO

BECAUSE...

MY WEEK WAS...

REMINDERS & NOTES:

a week of *gratitude* ♥

I AM GRATEFUL FOR ...

_____
_____
_____

I AM GRATEFUL FOR ...

_____
_____
_____

I AM GRATEFUL FOR ...

_____
_____
_____

I AM GRATEFUL FOR ...

_____
_____
_____

I AM GRATEFUL FOR ...

_____
_____
_____

I AM GRATEFUL FOR ...

_____
_____
_____

I AM GRATEFUL FOR ...

_____
_____
_____

WHAT I LEARNED THIS WEEK

_____
_____
_____

AFFIRMATION OF THE WEEK:

I FEEL ...

TO DO

BECAUSE...

MY WEEK WAS...

REMINDERS & NOTES:

a week of gratitude

I AM GRATEFUL FOR ...

I AM GRATEFUL FOR ...

I AM GRATEFUL FOR ...

I AM GRATEFUL FOR ...

I AM GRATEFUL FOR ...

I AM GRATEFUL FOR ...

I AM GRATEFUL FOR ...

WHAT I LEARNED THIS WEEK

AFFIRMATION OF THE WEEK:

I FEEL ...

TO DO

BECAUSE...

MY WEEK WAS...

REMINDERS & NOTES:

a week of gratitude ♥

I AM GRATEFUL FOR ...

I AM GRATEFUL FOR ...

I AM GRATEFUL FOR ...

I AM GRATEFUL FOR ...

I AM GRATEFUL FOR ...

I AM GRATEFUL FOR ...

I AM GRATEFUL FOR ...

WHAT I LEARNED THIS WEEK

AFFIRMATION OF THE WEEK:

I FEEL ...

TO DO

BECAUSE...

MY WEEK WAS...

REMINDERS & NOTES:

a week of *gratitude* ♥

I AM GRATEFUL FOR ...

I AM GRATEFUL FOR ...

I AM GRATEFUL FOR ...

I AM GRATEFUL FOR ...

I AM GRATEFUL FOR ...

I AM GRATEFUL FOR ...

I AM GRATEFUL FOR ...

WHAT I LEARNED THIS WEEK

AFFIRMATION OF THE WEEK:

I FEEL ...

TO DO

BECAUSE...

MY WEEK WAS...

REMINDERS & NOTES:

a week of gratitude

I AM GRATEFUL FOR ...

I AM GRATEFUL FOR ...

I AM GRATEFUL FOR ...

I AM GRATEFUL FOR ...

I AM GRATEFUL FOR ...

I AM GRATEFUL FOR ...

I AM GRATEFUL FOR ...

WHAT I LEARNED THIS WEEK

AFFIRMATION OF THE WEEK:

I FEEL ...

TO DO

BECAUSE...

MY WEEK WAS...

REMINDERS & NOTES:

a week of gratitude ♥

I AM GRATEFUL FOR ...

I AM GRATEFUL FOR ...

I AM GRATEFUL FOR ...

I AM GRATEFUL FOR ...

I AM GRATEFUL FOR ...

I AM GRATEFUL FOR ...

I AM GRATEFUL FOR ...

WHAT I LEARNED THIS WEEK

AFFIRMATION OF THE WEEK:

I FEEL ...   TO DO

BECAUSE...

MY WEEK WAS...

REMINDERS & NOTES:

a week of gratitude

I AM GRATEFUL FOR ...

I AM GRATEFUL FOR ...

I AM GRATEFUL FOR ...

I AM GRATEFUL FOR ...

I AM GRATEFUL FOR ...

I AM GRATEFUL FOR ...

I AM GRATEFUL FOR ...

WHAT I LEARNED THIS WEEK

AFFIRMATION OF THE WEEK:

I FEEL ...   TO DO

BECAUSE...

MY WEEK WAS...

REMINDERS & NOTES:

a week of gratitude ♥

I AM GRATEFUL FOR ...

_____
_____
_____

I AM GRATEFUL FOR ...

_____
_____
_____

I AM GRATEFUL FOR ...

_____
_____
_____

I AM GRATEFUL FOR ...

_____
_____
_____

I AM GRATEFUL FOR ...

_____
_____
_____

I AM GRATEFUL FOR ...

_____
_____
_____

I AM GRATEFUL FOR ...

_____
_____
_____

WHAT I LEARNED THIS WEEK

_____
_____
_____

AFFIRMATION OF THE WEEK:

I FEEL ...   TO DO

BECAUSE...

MY WEEK WAS...

REMINDERS & NOTES:

a week of gratitude ♥

I AM GRATEFUL FOR ...

I AM GRATEFUL FOR ...

I AM GRATEFUL FOR ...

I AM GRATEFUL FOR ...

I AM GRATEFUL FOR ...

I AM GRATEFUL FOR ...

I AM GRATEFUL FOR ...

WHAT I LEARNED THIS WEEK

AFFIRMATION OF THE WEEK:

I FEEL ...

TO DO

BECAUSE...

MY WEEK WAS...

REMINDERS & NOTES:

a week of gratitude ♥

I AM GRATEFUL FOR ...

I AM GRATEFUL FOR ...

I AM GRATEFUL FOR ...

I AM GRATEFUL FOR ...

I AM GRATEFUL FOR ...

I AM GRATEFUL FOR ...

I AM GRATEFUL FOR ...

WHAT I LEARNED THIS WEEK

AFFIRMATION OF THE WEEK:

I FEEL ...

TO DO

BECAUSE...

MY WEEK WAS...

REMINDERS & NOTES:

a week of gratitude

I AM GRATEFUL FOR ...

_____
_____
_____

I AM GRATEFUL FOR ...

_____
_____
_____

I AM GRATEFUL FOR ...

_____
_____
_____

I AM GRATEFUL FOR ...

_____
_____
_____

I AM GRATEFUL FOR ...

_____
_____
_____

I AM GRATEFUL FOR ...

_____
_____
_____

I AM GRATEFUL FOR ...

_____
_____
_____

WHAT I LEARNED THIS WEEK

_____
_____
_____

AFFIRMATION OF THE WEEK:

I FEEL ...

TO DO

BECAUSE...

MY WEEK WAS...

REMINDERS & NOTES:

a week of gratitude ♥

I AM GRATEFUL FOR ...

I AM GRATEFUL FOR ...

I AM GRATEFUL FOR ...

I AM GRATEFUL FOR ...

I AM GRATEFUL FOR ...

I AM GRATEFUL FOR ...

I AM GRATEFUL FOR ...

WHAT I LEARNED THIS WEEK

AFFIRMATION OF THE WEEK:

I FEEL ...

TO DO

BECAUSE...

MY WEEK WAS...

REMINDERS & NOTES:

a week of *gratitude* ♥

I AM GRATEFUL FOR …

_____
_____
_____

I AM GRATEFUL FOR …

_____
_____
_____

I AM GRATEFUL FOR …

_____
_____
_____

I AM GRATEFUL FOR …

_____
_____
_____

I AM GRATEFUL FOR …

_____
_____
_____

I AM GRATEFUL FOR …

_____
_____
_____

I AM GRATEFUL FOR …

_____
_____
_____

WHAT I LEARNED THIS WEEK

_____
_____
_____

AFFIRMATION OF THE WEEK:

I FEEL ...

TO DO

BECAUSE...

MY WEEK WAS...

REMINDERS & NOTES:

a week of gratitude ♥

I AM GRATEFUL FOR ...

_____
_____
_____

I AM GRATEFUL FOR ...

_____
_____
_____

I AM GRATEFUL FOR ...

_____
_____
_____

I AM GRATEFUL FOR ...

_____
_____
_____

I AM GRATEFUL FOR ...

_____
_____
_____

I AM GRATEFUL FOR ...

_____
_____
_____

I AM GRATEFUL FOR ...

_____
_____
_____

WHAT I LEARNED THIS WEEK

_____
_____
_____

AFFIRMATION OF THE WEEK:

I FEEL ...

TO DO

BECAUSE...

MY WEEK WAS...

REMINDERS & NOTES:

a week of *gratitude* ♥

I AM GRATEFUL FOR ...

I AM GRATEFUL FOR ...

I AM GRATEFUL FOR ...

I AM GRATEFUL FOR ...

I AM GRATEFUL FOR ...

I AM GRATEFUL FOR ...

I AM GRATEFUL FOR ...

WHAT I LEARNED THIS WEEK

AFFIRMATION OF THE WEEK:

I FEEL …

BECAUSE…

MY WEEK WAS…

TO DO

REMINDERS & NOTES:

a week of gratitude ♥

I AM GRATEFUL FOR ...

I AM GRATEFUL FOR ...

I AM GRATEFUL FOR ...

I AM GRATEFUL FOR ...

I AM GRATEFUL FOR ...

I AM GRATEFUL FOR ...

I AM GRATEFUL FOR ...

WHAT I LEARNED THIS WEEK

AFFIRMATION OF THE WEEK:

I FEEL …

BECAUSE…

MY WEEK WAS…

TO DO

REMINDERS & NOTES:

a week of gratitude

I AM GRATEFUL FOR ...

I AM GRATEFUL FOR ...

I AM GRATEFUL FOR ...

I AM GRATEFUL FOR ...

I AM GRATEFUL FOR ...

I AM GRATEFUL FOR ...

I AM GRATEFUL FOR ...

WHAT I LEARNED THIS WEEK

AFFIRMATION OF THE WEEK:

I FEEL ...

BECAUSE...

MY WEEK WAS...

TO DO

REMINDERS & NOTES:

a week of gratitude ♥

I AM GRATEFUL FOR ...

I AM GRATEFUL FOR ...

I AM GRATEFUL FOR ...

I AM GRATEFUL FOR ...

I AM GRATEFUL FOR ...

I AM GRATEFUL FOR ...

I AM GRATEFUL FOR ...

WHAT I LEARNED THIS WEEK

AFFIRMATION OF THE WEEK:

I FEEL ...

TO DO

BECAUSE...

MY WEEK WAS...

REMINDERS & NOTES:

a week of gratitude ♥

I AM GRATEFUL FOR ...

I AM GRATEFUL FOR ...

I AM GRATEFUL FOR ...

I AM GRATEFUL FOR ...

I AM GRATEFUL FOR ...

I AM GRATEFUL FOR ...

I AM GRATEFUL FOR ...

WHAT I LEARNED THIS WEEK

AFFIRMATION OF THE WEEK:

I FEEL ...

TO DO

BECAUSE...

MY WEEK WAS...

REMINDERS & NOTES:

a week of gratitude

I AM GRATEFUL FOR ...

I AM GRATEFUL FOR ...

I AM GRATEFUL FOR ...

I AM GRATEFUL FOR ...

I AM GRATEFUL FOR ...

I AM GRATEFUL FOR ...

I AM GRATEFUL FOR ...

WHAT I LEARNED THIS WEEK

AFFIRMATION OF THE WEEK:

I FEEL ...

TO DO

BECAUSE...

MY WEEK WAS...

REMINDERS & NOTES:

a week of gratitude ♥

I AM GRATEFUL FOR …

I AM GRATEFUL FOR …

I AM GRATEFUL FOR …

I AM GRATEFUL FOR …

I AM GRATEFUL FOR …

I AM GRATEFUL FOR …

I AM GRATEFUL FOR …

WHAT I LEARNED THIS WEEK

AFFIRMATION OF THE WEEK:

I FEEL ...

TO DO

BECAUSE...

MY WEEK WAS...

REMINDERS & NOTES:

a week of *gratitude* ♥

I AM GRATEFUL FOR ...

_____
_____
_____

I AM GRATEFUL FOR ...

_____
_____
_____

I AM GRATEFUL FOR ...

_____
_____
_____

I AM GRATEFUL FOR ...

_____
_____
_____

I AM GRATEFUL FOR ...

_____
_____
_____

I AM GRATEFUL FOR ...

_____
_____
_____

I AM GRATEFUL FOR ...

_____
_____
_____

WHAT I LEARNED THIS WEEK

_____
_____
_____

© 2020
Vanessa Stark
Untergasse 3
61118 Bad Vilbel

www.vanessastark.de

CPSIA information can be obtained
at www.ICGtesting.com
Printed in the USA
LVHW080016091220
673675LV00051B/1715